MW00655828

# A Bartender's View of Life

## 101 Things You Sure Didn't Learn in School

By Walt Coffey

Printed and edited by
Tom Leathers Publishing
4500 College Blvd., Leawood, KS 66206

Printed by Tom Leathers Publishing, 4500 College Blvd., Leawood, KS 66211. Phone (913) 498-2625, Fax (913) 498-1561.

Designed by Margaret Dalke of Leathers Publishing.

Photos by Carol Coffey.

Cover photo by J. Miller Summers Photography.

## *Dedicated to*

*— all the great friends, relatives and customers who supported my efforts in the Longbranch and life. They stuck with me during the victories and the dregs. They know who they are, and I can't express enough Thank Yous. To the rest of you I will place a whammy that I learned in a tattoo shop in Bombay during a hurricane. Read this and expect your hair to fall out soon. Revenge is sweet!*

# Table of Contents

*(A page for every problem)*

# FOREWORD

In these pages you will find a collection of short sayings about the adventures in our daily lives.

As an active saloon owner, I am afforded a rare opportunity to see and hear of various situations as they unfold, with both their humor and sadness. This is material not taught in schools, but perhaps should be.

These one-liners are posted at random on the walls of the Longbranch Steakhouse Saloon located at 9095 Metcalf in Overland Park, Kansas, an upscale suburb of Kansas City.

I'm there every day, keeping abreast of the business and my many customers and friends. I'm personally inviting you to come by, and together we can add an insightful saying to the "Walls of fame."

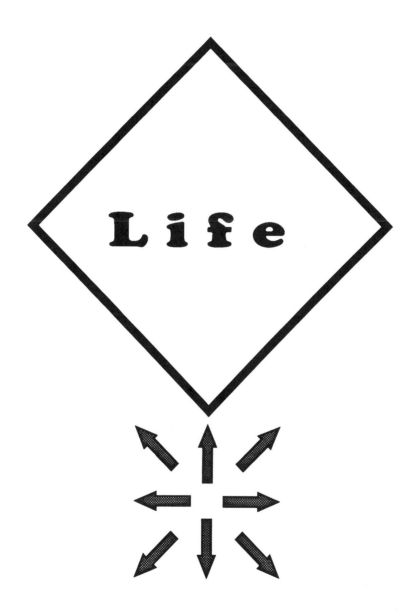

**All gamblers die broke**

Simple, yet true. It matters not how frequently they win, nor the amount, for Dr. Doom lurks around every corner for the bettor. People who wager remember and talk about the days they win, ignoring the numerous losses, and never divulging the many times Dr. Doom strikes, defeating them. Have you noticed they always keep their day job? I wonder why, considering their winnings.

**If something in the mail says you've won, you haven't**

Where in the world is Ed McMahon? His presence is desperately needed at my house. I continue to purchase magazines from the mailings that indicate I am surely a big winner. They are very elaborate and official-looking, hard to say no to, even as reading material takes over my house. Ed McMahon, where are you and where is my money? I want it!

**Always blame someone who is unable to defend himself**

Great philosophy, especially effective when the poor soul being held responsible is not present to protect himself.

I have personally observed and used this method on numerous occasions, and it is highly successful if you keep the door locked so he cannot take part in the meeting. Later, when you have a chance encounter with your helpless victim in the hall, try not to appear like the dirty rat back-stabber you really are.

An alcoholic is someone who drinks more than his doctor

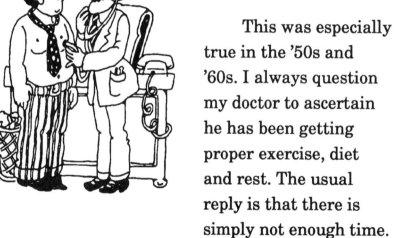

This was especially true in the '50s and '60s. I always question my doctor to ascertain he has been getting proper exercise, diet and rest. The usual reply is that there is simply not enough time. Where does he think I'll get the time when I spend so much of it in his waiting room? Couldn't he buy up-to-date magazines?

**"As good as" means "it isn't."**

Save yourself aggravation, just purchase the original instead of the "As good as." How are we to determine if it's really as good until we purchase it and find out it isn't.

I also worry when a product boasts of being "new and improved." Are they admitting it was not up to snuff a year ago? Are they informing me I was using bad judgment when I purchased the old product?

# Bills will rise to meet increased income

Actually, bills rise at a pace slightly below the speed of sound, while income increases at the rate of slow-growing grass. It is one of the laws of the universe, and no one has quite figured it out. It will continue to baffle wage earners throughout the civilized world. Save in this area, and something will surely break down in another, vacuuming the savings plus an additional 10%. Raises are set at 3% a year, while six packs go up 20%. It's the law, written to keep you in the bondage of the poorhouse.

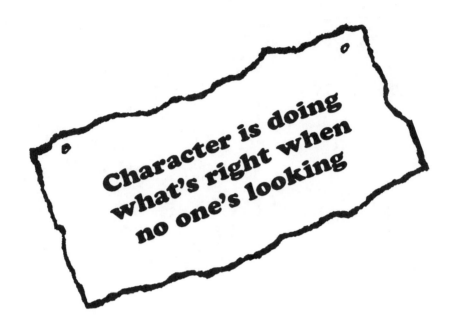

**Character is doing what's right when no one's looking**

What a terrific description of a simple way to conduct oneself through life. Problem is, persons who put the program into daily use seem to go unnoticed; it's the schmucks we read about. Just do the right thing; you will sleep better and develop better friendships. Your food will taste better, and you will get fat.

**Don't look back — we ain't goin' that way!**

Not only is this the gospel truth, it is an excellent philosophy to govern your life by, especially for those of us who tend to make an excessive amount of wrong turns. Dump the luggage of the past, embark on a bright new future and, of course, a new set of bad decisions.

**Forgive, but don't forget**

To forgive is both noble and kind of you, but to forget is just plain stupid. Don't let the bum borrow your car again. Last time he brought it back on empty and filthy. Why don't you lend 'em your credit card this time. I'm sure you will be elated with the result, and you can pay it over five years.

**Greener grass has hidden weeds**

This is a fact of life from which there is no escape. All things when first observed somehow manage to show only the glamorous side. Realism usually takes time to arrive. You can't see the lady's wrinkles in a dark bar, and she won't be able to tell you have a big beer gut. Join a health club and clean up your act, or don't be seen in daylight.

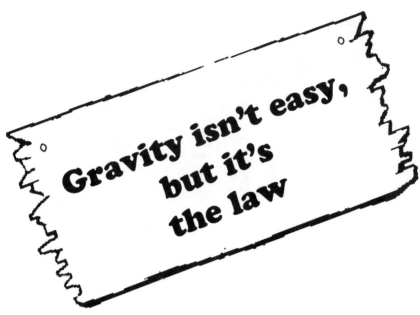

# Gravity isn't easy, but it's the law

What about all those rules we seldom like or agree with? Who the heck wants to drive 55 on a super highway with four lanes and no traffic? And what about repealing the law that makes you hit your hurt finger on just about everything? Gravity helps you fall apart physically as you age — kinda makes things droop that you wish would stay put. Perhaps standing on your head one hour per day would cause reverse offsetting droop and cancel the problem.

## How come one-hour dry cleaners need 3 days?

Am I missing something? Recently I checked a suit in for dry cleaning in a shop with a sign proudly hawking "One-Hour Service." The clerk handed me my numbered receipt and informed me I could retrieve my clothing in 3 days. There is a huge difference between 1 hour and 3 days if you happen to be a suit. I'd sure enjoy meeting the guy who thinks up those signs, surely a fiendish type who takes great joy in our confusion.

There are things we must accept in life; this is one. It's also the reason I walk around in a soiled, wrinkled suit.

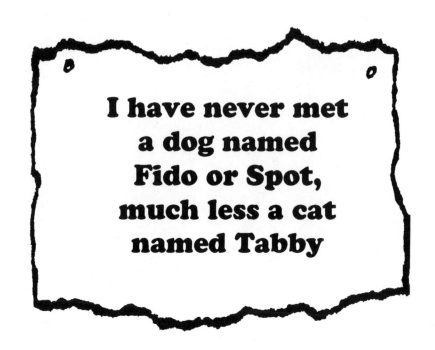

I have never met
a dog named
Fido or Spot,
much less a cat
named Tabby

Do you find it strange, all that stuff my first reader was about.

"See Jack throw the ball to Spot. See Spot bring the ball to Jane. See Jane throw the ball to Dick. See Spot try to kill Tabby."

It was great reading, do you recall it the way I do?

I would not want to belong to any club or organization that would have a person like me as a member.

An intelligent appraisal emitting from one who has honestly assessed his own character. I believe Groucho said it. I will always fondly remember Groucho as host of "You Bet Your Life," black and white TV at its best. He would sit there leering at his female guests, cigar in hand, making sure they won something, with questions like "Who was the George Washington Bridge named after?" and who can forget, "Say the right word and watch the duck drop"? Corny as hell, but unforgettable. I want him in my club.

**If you have not seen this sign, tell the bartender; win a free drink.**

Gotcha — this sign behind the bar is one of my personal favorites — and the perfect catch 22. For years I have enjoyed watching customers attempt to qualify for a free drink. Their first attempt is always "I haven't seen that sign." Dueling with them can make the bartender a target for countless ploys which he always fends off.

Why don't you drop by and take a shot at winning a free drink?

? FREE ?

Could be my favorite saying, I wish I'd thought of it. It's for everyone who departed some town or city badly, either for financial or personal reasons. The scene is clear, my hero walking down the street with the town folks hitting him with rotten tomatoes and cursing him. But my hero is smiling and waving at the crowd. My kind of guy!

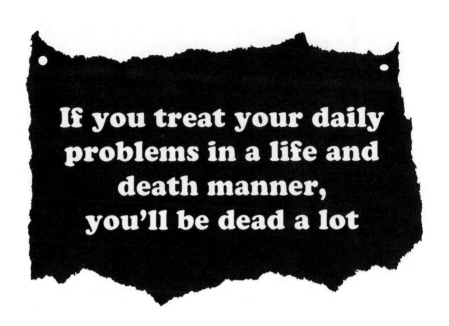

**If you treat your daily problems in a life and death manner, you'll be dead a lot**

Do you have a friend or relative who makes each negative event a terrible, hand-wringing crisis? Worse yet, are you that person? Admit it if you are. I have known many of these poor folks, nice otherwise, but they see every negative event as an end to life. Didn't anyone inform them that tires go flat, kids don't listen and all roofs eventually leak. This is why God invented bartenders. They can offer a solution to any problem, no matter how vexing.

# In case of fire, yell fire

Too simple, you're thinking, it's a dumb saying; you are wrong. Well, consider how some jerks can overcomplicate about 80% of the instructions you attempt to read and interpret. Who writes those things, are they trying to torture us? Apparently they are. Is it possible that we are facing a pinko commie plan to overthrow the United States by screwing up otherwise simple instructions?

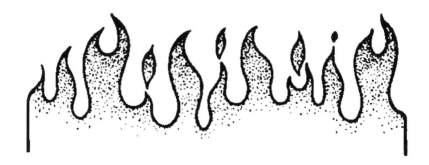

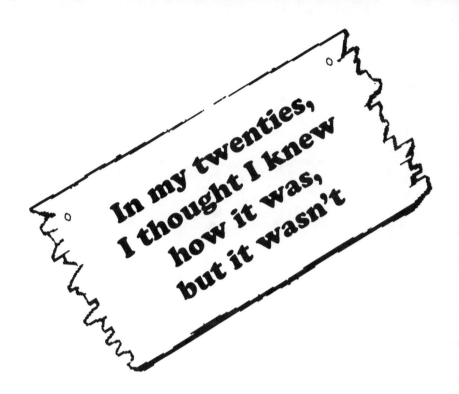

**In my twenties, I thought I knew how it was, but it wasn't**

Certainly wasn't, not even close. Relationships, finances, parental advice, almost nothing worked the way it should. Me, have a beer gut — never. I'd never be broke, never be gray. "I'd fight and never lose" — that's what the song said, and I believed it.

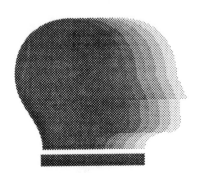

Don't listen to that song, for it will lead you down the primrose path, if you have not already been there.

**It's what you learn after you know it ALL that counts**

Try selling that truism to most 18-year-olds. Instead, just put on a helmet and run into a brick wall — six times. It will be a far easier task. Then your 18-year-old kid can go out to the pool hall where he belongs on a school night. Most kids say they are going to the library. You told it to your folks. Admit all the things you did wrong to your kids. You don't dare, do you?

# It ain't hard to be at your best if you stink

It can at times be relaxing to realize you are simply terrible at a particular task. Once you adopt this mindset, there is no need to play golf the way many at the local clubs do — cheating, frustrated and cursing each bad shot. They have yet to figure out that their good days are the accidents, and the bad days are their real game. Relax, have fun, stink, lose money, have a beer.

**It takes a smart man to know he's dumb**

We are all acquainted with a few no-brain personalities who loudly profess considerable knowledge on any subject that may arise. Once you have unmasked them, slink away into the night, hoping to encounter someone of reasonable intelligence, or at least someone smart enough to know he doesn't know.
Hope this makes sense.
I checked it out with
a smart guy before I
wrote it.

# It's better to be sad in a limo than on a bus

Pretty much true, recalling a vacation in Ft. Lauderdale when I managed to travel in each mode. I was transported in style in the Marriott Hotel limo to beautiful Gulf Stream track, one of the really classy horse racing facilities in the U.S. When the races ended for the day, my billfold was empty, and except for pocket change I was busted due to astute betting. The return ride on the hot, dirty bus was quite a contrast to my glorious arrival.

**It's better to receive than give**

There is an art to doing this without getting caught. You must carefully monitor the value of gifts received and make sure the value of gifts given is 20% less. This requires planning and deceit, but if properly executed can result in a nice profit. Remember, save all the empty boxes from expensive stores, and you're on your way. You better not try to fool me, but good luck with others. It's every man for himself!

It's easier to lower your standard of living than it is to make more money

You're darn tootin' it is. If you persuade the boss to give you a $1000-a-year raise, what is left after taxes will quickly evaporate in a pile of bills. An easier plan would be to purchase a cheaper car and spend your time in less expensive restaurants, like mine, of course. If you can manage to

accomplish all of the above, you may wind up wealthy, and hopefully share some of it with me. Send me some money. I need it.

I spent 90% of my money on whiskey, gambling and women and wasted the rest

I personally have known and observed dozens of guys who lived by this rule. They seemed to enjoy themselves despite the fact that they appeared about 60 on their 40th birthday. The lifestyle is similar to getting a reverse facelift, or trying to develop a beer gut and attain poverty. They usually manage to achieve all of these things.

Intelligence has boundaries, but dumb is seemingly limitless

How many times at various functions must you endure the blabber of a brainless wonder? Thank God for brew and pubs containing booths to escape these otherwise nice people.

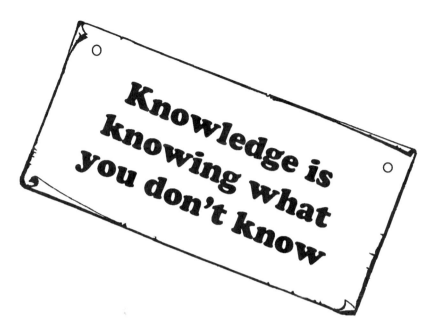

**Knowledge is knowing what you don't know**

Take a moment and think back, remembering the advice you were given by persons who did not have the faintest idea what they were talking about. However well intended, their advice can screw you up, which is something you should reserve the right to do yourself. Then, lucky enough to reach old age, you can attempt to impart knowledge about life to someone as hard-headed as you were.

**Life is too serious to be taken seriously**

Sure as heck is. Remember, 60% of your problems will melt away with time. Deal with what you can change and wish the rest on your worst enemy. It is actually possible that placing a curse on your enemy can cause transfer. But it must be done naked in front of a full moon, preferably not on a busy street.

## Most of the disasters in my life never occurred

Worry, worry, worry. It would be very nice if I could regain the time I spent worrying about problems that never occurred. Certainly we've all heard the adage "Only worry about things you can control!" True, simple, but oh so tough to do. Spring is in the air, and it is time for me to start worrying about how the K.C. baseball team will fare, wonder if my roof will leak, the stock market could crash. It could be a bad year, perhaps a terrible one. Is there a shrink in the house?

**Never help anyone move**

What a terrible trap, set to snare unwary folks: "We're having a moving party, drop by and help with a few boxes. By the way, bring your moving van." Three warm beers and five hours later, you start to curse yourself for being suckered in. Next time you're invited, use any excuse that comes to your mind to avoid this event. In fact, having a root canal done that day is preferable to attending this miserable sadistic ritual.

Never buy a used car from a man in a plaid coat — named Slick

The mere thought of purchasing a used car causes otherwise strong people to break out in a cold sweat; their knees feel weak. You feel dumb, not knowing anything about trade-ins, financing, mechanics, prices, etc. Determined not to make a bad buy, you research, even reading my special chapter on how to buy a used car. Now you're tough, confident, armed with facts, ready to face the world of used cars. You drive to the nearby dealer, and out comes the salesman, named Slick — wearing a plaid coat — smoking a cigar — a big diamond on his hand — you go back home.

*See Article on Used Cars (Page 145)*

# Never buy anything that needs assembling

We have all been trapped by the simple words, "Easy to assemble. Two tools required." I recently attempted to install an undersink water purifier that calls for 10-minute assembly. Forty-five minutes later, while wading in my kitchen, I contacted the plumber, who (lucky for me) came out quickly and in 30 minutes completed the installation. The $30 water purifier was working after paying the plumber $93. Have you been there? Have you cursed yourself for falling for the "easy to assemble" bait? Surely you had an argument with your wonderful spouse over the meaning of the instructions. You're as big a sucker as I am.

Nothing is
impossible if
someone else
has to do it

A wonderful system, especially adaptable for sales managers and coaches everywhere. I utilize it when we are about to have a very busy evening in the restaurant, simply saying a silent prayer that I will not be called on to step in and assist them, fearful of being unmasked as the inept fraud I am. Never let 'em see you sweat.

# Never trust anyone who says "Trust me"

The dirty rat, varment, scum bag who utters those words is about to fleece you, or worse. A person you can trust would never say that, wouldn't need to. Only those with a sinister motive would utter those words, and they are also the type who drive cars with darkly tinted windows so you can't peep inside — to see what the hell is going on and with whom.

## One man's trash is another man's trash

Come on, trash is trash! Show me a junky car
that some kid spends all his money fixing up, and
I'll show you a disguised junker. You'll notice the
repair bills that always remind you. Trash is pretty
much trash, but if that's what you like, keep it all.
Your spouse will love looking at it as it fills the
basement, then seems to grow on the garage walls.
When you move, you can review it all and say,
"When the hell did we get all this stuff?"

## Sober people break legs

Moderate drinkers just seem to fall down better. They hang a little looser. I get a phone call, late at night. The caller informs me, "Mac, your lawyer just broke his leg." I question the caller, "Good for him, was he sober?" The reply is affirmative; he hadn't had a drink, and my theory is once again proven in real life. Too bad he did not have a few drinks at my place first. He would never have broken his leg, just skinned his knee. We would have given him first aid, a beer and a band-aid.

Some people
are not happy
unless they
are not happy

We are all acquainted with a few of these poor souls. I have a friend, a kindly, likeable guy who, when questioned about how things are going, simply bows his head, moves it slowly back and forth negatively and says, "I'm getting by, but it's rough." That's on his good days. I don't dare ask him anything when I know he's having a **bad** day. Next time we meet I'll just greet him with, "Sorry you're havin' a lousy day, tomorrow will be worse!"

# Teamwork allows you to blame someone else

Rarely in my 30 years in business did someone say, "I screwed up the program." Nearly everyone is convinced the other people involved allowed the breakdown of the plan. At all times assemble a large enough group to allow you to blame the person least likely to defend his position.

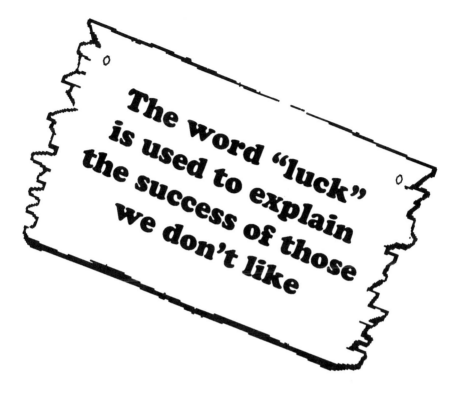

The word "luck" is used to explain the success of those we don't like

Come on, don't give those you don't care for the credit they deserve. The rule is to find a way to discredit their accomplishments. Always infer they were "in the right place at the right time." Another good way to knock them down is by stating "they fell into a sewer and came out smelling like a rose." Telling lies and starting rumors at cocktail parties can be especially effective. Intimate you have startling facts, but their source must remain secret.

Good job!

# The payments seem higher as the car gets older

You sure do enjoy the new car smell, right? Wrong, unless you value it about $10,000 the first year, and that's about $800 a month. After that, the smell disappears and goes to new car smell heaven, never to return. At this point you have a large car payment for years to come, but a used car smell. And on top of the big payment, you must contend with the scratch on the left fender that mysteriously appeared when your child used the vehicle. Of course, he denies it, and he is such a saintly person. Only 38 payments left on this dented, stinky, used car.

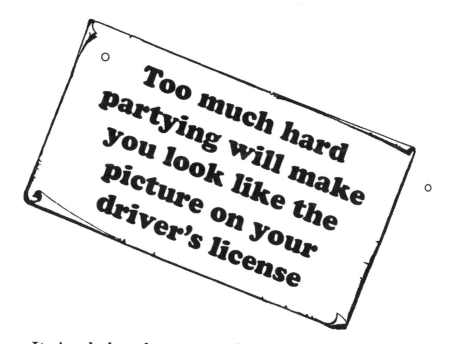

Too much hard partying will make you look like the picture on your driver's license

It simply boggles my mind that anyone could operate a camera in such a manner as to make pictures turn out so stinkin' bad. The result could be used for blackmail if you so desired. Did he use a distorted lens as a joke and laugh at the results later? Don't you just cringe when asked to present your driver's license? It's enough to make you discontinue writing checks, much less get caught speeding. Of course, you could say it's a picture of you when you were older. Try hard to look better than that license picture, or don't be seen in public in daylight.

You're having a long day when the woman in the check-out line in front of you produces coupons and a check book

Come on, can't they pass a law against these people? Shouldn't they have a special line for them? Didn't this normal 45-year-old woman know she'd need her driver's license when she wrote the check? I purchased a house quicker than some folks check out. Standing behind them, I glare at the back of their head, but they refuse to turn around and face me. At least, the forever wait gives me the opportunity to read the scandal tabloids and find out who's doing what to whom. You people from hell know who you are. Admit it and repent. I hope your shopping cart loses a wheel.

**Pessimists never get disappointed**

Heck, no, they don't. They open a business assuming they will go broke and end up on welfare. When the transmission breaks in their car, they know it was about time. I think next year I'll try their methods. It's about time my roof started to leak, it's three years old. It is very difficult to ruin a pessimist's day.

The valet who just parked your car does not work here

Now isn't that a cheerful thought as you hand the keys to your new Vette convertible to a stranger, and as you turn to head to your destination hear the squeal of tires. When the smiling guy sticks out his hand for my keys, I hand 'em over as if he had a gun and tip him a dollar just hopin' he's on my side. Of course, I drive cars no one wants to steal, so I'm relatively safe, but you'd better watch out.

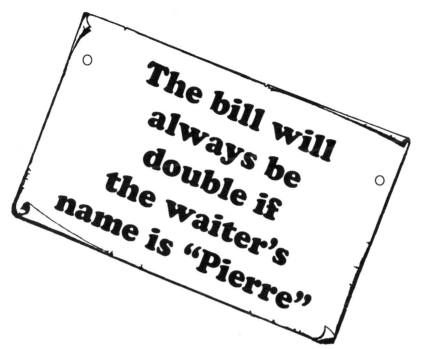

**The bill will always be double if the waiter's name is "Pierre"**

Brace yourself and have your unlimited charge card ready when you see the tab from this guy. It seems to be an unwritten law in the restaurant industry that Pierres work in pricey joints and are simply not allowed in Duke's burger and beer joint. If Pierre served it, rest assured it will have a blue sauce with things you have never seen around the edges. As for me, grill the onions, send a cold Bud, and see if Molly can be my server tonight.

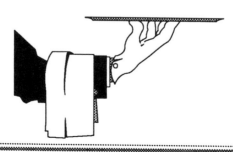

## The line you're not in moves faster

You're ready for the trip to the grocery, even have the list you can't read on a scrap of paper. (What does "blat" mean?) You deftly move through the aisles, then pick the shortest check-out. There's a lady with only 10 items, should be quick. She rings out, surveys the bill and pulls out six coupons. The clerk refigures the bill, and now she produces a checkbook.

"You need my driver's license? I could not possibly know that. I'm only 48 and have been writing checks 20 years." No woman wants to show the picture on her license; it's reason enough to pay cash.

I glare at her, she glares back. War is hell!

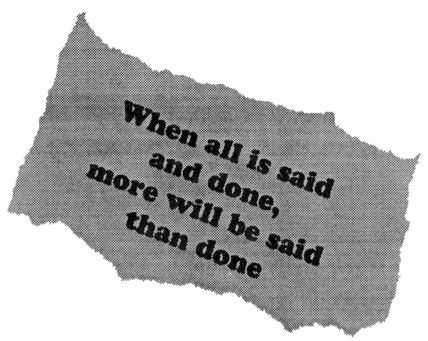

When all is said
and done,
more will be said
than done

I have attended and slept through numerous meetings and get-togethers in several careers, far too many to recall 'em all, but one fact consistently emerges. Many persons are somehow involved in what one 10th grader could accomplish in half the time for only a promise to use the family car Saturday night. If the truth were known and admitted, the entire agenda could be assigned to the 10th grader, and we would have saved the two dozen glazed doughnuts purchased for the event. Bring your kid to the next important meeting.

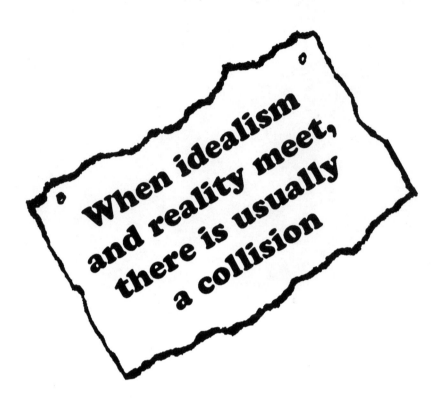

When idealism and reality meet, there is usually a collision

This is a fact of life which generally occurs between the ages of 18 and death, when an individual on his or her own and stripped of capital, has his or her face shoved in the dirt of the real world. The world is tougher than most of us would like to believe, and some would lead you to the garden, turn you over to the snake and split. Chances are, if you think about it, a name will surface who attempted to do it to you. Hang onto your values, but don't leave your keys in the car.

# Why does "One Hour Photo" take 8 hours?

Last Monday about high noon I delivered the undeveloped roll of film for processing. The friendly lady behind the counter handed me the receipt, informing me the prints could be picked up after 8 p.m. that evening. I politely pointed to the "One Hour" sign. She simply smiled and went about doing whatever it is good clerks do. There are all sorts of mysteries in life we must accept; they are simply too big to fight. This is one!

Try this: Yell at the clerk and say, "I want my film in one hour." Good luck!

Wise men have something intelligent to say, but fools simply must say something

I don't know the person who penned this insightful saying, but I imagine he spent considerable time in local pubs, each with at least one group who gather regularly. We refer to them as the table of wisdom, and though they are nice guys, they could cause global warming with the hot air they produce. There is not one subject in which they are not expert. It boggles the mind the problems they think they solve.

**Women are like streetcars; the ocean's full of 'em**

Numerous customers inquire as to what this means. Frankly, I don't have the vaguest idea, but it sounds profound. As I recall, Archie Bunker uttered it, and we are aware of his twisted wisdom. Remember this one and tell it to your kids.

# You know you're in a good neighborhood if you don't have to pay for your gas first

Conversely, if the sign on the pump says, "Please pay inside before fueling," you have just been informed that you are in a less-than-safe environment and should get the hell out of the area as quickly as your vehicle will allow, burning rubber so to speak. The Lone Ranger yelled, "Hi, ho, Silver," and ran away from trouble. In this situation you should think of yourself as the Ranger and make a rapid move to the highway with your windows up and your doors locked.

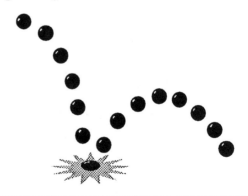

# You don't need to say a lot to say a lot

Sad but true, we all meet the big blabber mouths. They ruin a lot of otherwise mellow evenings, and you could record everything they said that was intelligent into two minutes of tape. Just pretend you're listening but excuse yourself to make a fake phone call. Tell 'em you need to pick someone up at the airport and split. They will be talking when you return, and probably will not have missed you.

# Aging

## How come everyone at the reunion looked older than you?

Come on, confess. You and your best friend from school sat at a reunion table making comments like, "My god, look how she's aged, and look at him. I'd have never known him if it weren't for the name tag and toupee." It is certain you and your friend have escaped the ravages of time, congratulations? By the way, the gang at the corner table are saying the same thing about you. See 'em pointing and laughing, and it's not at what you're wearing. You are turning into an old geezer.

# Under Old Management

I feel safe and secure with been-around-a-long-time management. The "new" infers the company was out of sync. A mature guiding hand infers the company is operating in a comfortable groove.

My five favorite restaurants are well established, rather than the new, glitzy, stand-in-line-an-hour type. I must admit I drive a nine-year-old brown four-door that thieves couldn't care less for. There is nothing more comforting than discovering an old neighborhood hardware store. There is always some nice old guy who can tell you how to fix your sink, and will sell you just two bolts.

You know you're getting old when the fortune teller wants to read your face

Certainly she would prefer to read your face, there's a heck of a lot more lines there to interpret. Take pride in the fact that you are older (unless mature sounds better), wiser and vastly more confused.

> # You know you're getting old when your muscles are sore from <u>NOT</u> working out.

You should witness my older friends wander into my saloon for a beer or five. They limp along, appearing to have just completed a one-hour military exercise drill. About all that seems to work well is their elbow when they lift a beer. Their drinking arm does not seem to develop soreness or arthritis; it's the rest of their body that goes to hell.

# You're not just getting older, you're getting worse

Certain as night follows day, you're becoming an old geezer or geezerette, as the case may be. You can purchase work-out machines in volume from TV informercials, but the law of gravity will cause everything to droop. It's simply too big to fight, too big a hill to climb for one who appears as young as you perceive yourself. You're over the hill, geezer; quit fighting it, enroll in AARP and take the geezer discount in restaurants and airlines. Regardless of what you think, you do not appear too young for the discount.

**You know you're getting old when you want to paint the town beige**

It's a fact! Do I enjoy painting it beige? I tremble at the thought of accompanying any person who looks remotely like he intends to have a big night on the town. Always take your own transportation and an airtight excuse to exit early. Some good lies to tell are: "I need to pick up a friend at the airport" or "I'm getting a root canal at 6 a.m." Get the hell out of there before fun happens. Fun can be a lot of work.

You know you're getting old when you look forward to a dull evening

The rewards of a quiet evening, with nothing on the agenda, can be enjoyable. There is no necessity to converse. Your brain is at rest, and you need not act like you're having a good time. Having a good time requires money, energy and a constant smile. It can wear your face out.

# Your Friendly Banker?

# A banker will only loan you money if you can prove you don't need it

Question just about anyone who ever attempted to obtain his first business loan. Then step back as he unloads his woes. At the start you happily enter the bank, having seen the ad with the pretty smiling lady informing you the bank was anxious to lend your business start-up money, fast and easy.

Instead of meeting her, you encounter a moderately smiling, stern-type woman who hands you 110 forms and instructs you to dare not return until they are filled out, warning you they better be correct.

One month later, walking slower now, you slink into the bank and hand the papers to — guess who — the loan officer. This non-smiling guy looks like he is on parole, probably is. It is time to yell, "I want to see the pretty smiling lady from the ad."

If it works, let me know!

Would a banker evict a widow with three kids — on Christmas Eve — in a snow storm? Of course!

Sure, he would, and then chuckle about it at the next staff meeting. How come bankers always discuss bad loans at expensive lunches. Just doesn't seem right. At board meetings they plot and plan the next ad campaign, using that pretty smiling lady to lure you in, then confront you with the mean, stern lady who orders you to sit and wait, usually a long time. And you better do it. The only reading material to browse while waiting is the *Wall Street Journal.* I'm quite sure they would have *Playboy,* but the president wants it in his office. Just go knock on his door and ask to borrow it.

Live it up, have some fun!

# Religion

Almighty God
Heaven
Zip Unknown

Dear God:

I just wanted to let you know that I respect your various ministers and churches, though I often wonder if you play favorites. On the following pages I am simply giving them a good-natured ribbing and have no desire to irritate anyone, especially you. The last thing I want to do is dodge lightning bolts on a sunny day. Hope you enjoy the book and let your pals in on it.

Best wishes,
*Walt*

P.S. I met the devil a few times and admit listening to him, but don't like him. I told him to get lost, get out of town and don't come back.

My minister said money can't buy happiness, but he seems overjoyed to get mine

If you have watched enough TV, I'm sure you've observed the many ministers sweatin', yellin' and tellin' us our worldly possessions have no meaning, we should unload them. Just about the time you're ready to live in a tent, they start cryin' that only money — yours — can save 'em. They also have problems. Funds are desperately needed to pay their limo drivers, maid and personal pilot. They conveniently forget to mention their air-conditioned dog house. It seems your money can buy happiness if you give it to them.

Be a happy person, go live in a tent without a toilet!

# Church is where you can talk about good deeds without having to do them

I was raised Catholic and attended a Catholic grade school where the nuns regularly whacked us with rulers and other dangerous weapons.

Much of my early years was spent dodging and defending myself. In those days I believed all those folks attending church every Sunday had some special pull with God and were superior to everyone else.

Then I became old enough (14) to frequent the local pubs. These same folks seemed to think God could not see 'em there. They were invisible as it was dimly lit and smoky. They became mere mortals or worse, if that's possible, right before my eyes.

My bartender gave me a different perspective, and his was about right on target.

Only a minister can condense a 10-minute sermon into 30 minutes

What's going on here; how long can ministers make a single thought last? What in the world are they trying to accomplish? Why don't they just sum up the thought, adjourn and let's go have coffee and doughnuts in the back of the church. It's a terrific spot to start nasty rumors about the lady across the room. It's the same one whose windows you peeked in with your telescope in the interest of neighborhood safety, unlike some pervert.

If you can chat with the preacher, you can feel like something rubbed off and you are somehow superior to your neighbor who is sitting home drinking beer, under a tree, listening to country music.

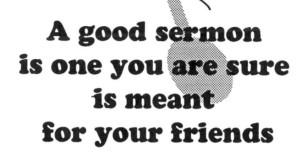

**A good sermon
is one you are sure
is meant
for your friends**

Certainly the preacher can't be referring to you; he probably means the widow Nancy who lives next door. Seems she has been arriving home late several times a week and laughter can be overheard, sounds bad. She keeps the blinds drawn, making it very difficult for you to peer in with the telescope you told your kids you purchased to study the planet Mars.

You can start some ugly rumors in church next Sunday. Have you ever considered purchasing the new ultra-sound equipment? Lets you hear through walls, might even discover a pervert in the neighborhood, stickin' his nose where it doesn't belong.

# Politics

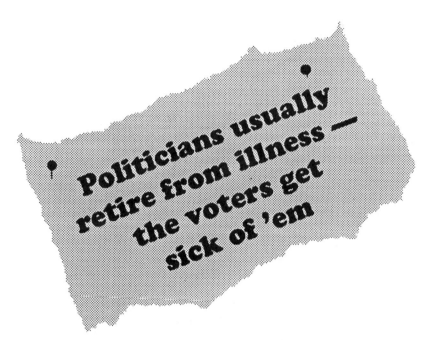

Politicians usually retire from illness — the voters get sick of 'em

The politicians in D.C. claim they are our public servants, right? Wrong! Problem with that theory is they pay themselves about five times what the average American earns, plus a fat expense account. And this doesn't even count the graft. Worse yet, they vote for their own raises.

Something is upside down and all screwed up. Whoever heard of a system like that in real life. Write 'em, tell 'em you want the same medical coverage and retirement benefits they vote themselves.

Fat chance! It's darned obvious the animals are running the zoo.

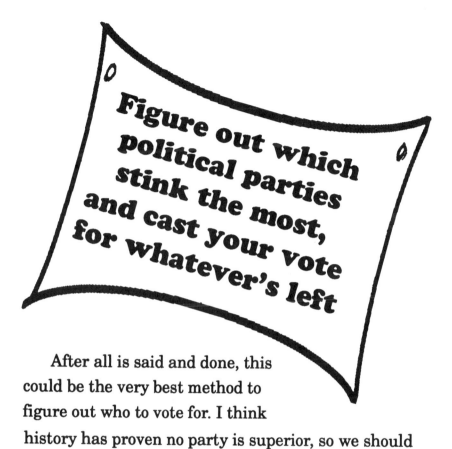

Figure out which
political parties
stink the most,
and cast your vote
for whatever's left

After all is said and done, this
could be the very best method to
figure out who to vote for. I think
history has proven no party is superior, so we should
use my famous bad apple theory.

Throw out the rotten apples first, but realize that
the remaining fruit will get lousy in a short time.

The folks we send to Washington have proven my
famous apple theory to work without fail. We need a
better system, but until we develop
one I believe this will work as well
as anything.

This whole mess in Washington is
way over my head.

# Marriage

Divorce can make you a millionaire if you begin with two million

Ah, yes, the financial pitfalls of marital bliss, especially when the lawyers get into the final act. It now becomes necessary to support not only your new home and your ex's residence, but also your attorney's house, and his is probably nicer than yours. Divorce can be a rather rough experience, sometimes causing you to live in your car. Marriage by itself is reason to consider owning a station wagon or van. Better yet, a camper, with beer and a TV.

Remember the Boy Scout motto, "Always be prepared." That motto could possibly be modified to "Always be single."

## Don't go to bed mad — stay up and fight

It would be interesting to meet the expert who thought up this bit of life's wisdom. You can easily picture 50% of the married people walking around their various work places, bleary-eyed, looking like zombies because they debated the battle of the sexes far into the night. It's obvious the person who penned the saying was single, and rested. Better take my advice, get a good night's sleep, the problem will wait for you, like a snake in the grass.

# Guys get married when they get tired of holding their stomachs in

These days after they say "I do," everything starts to go to hell. The stomach protrudes, showers and shaves get fewer, and romantic dinners absolutely end. That's the main reason they got married. There was a slob inside waiting to emerge. You never should have married the bum. Get on the

phone, call your mother and tell her she was right all along. Better yet, pack up, move back home with your folks and mooch off them. Life will be easy there; you can lay around eating pizza, make your mom wait on you and get money from your dad.

Anyone who ever had the misfortune to design and build a house is aware of this saying. The ladies are obviously hell-bent on destroying us financially. The men, on the other hand, are conservative by nature and would never waste the family resources on an expensive riding mower for a small yard. It's apparent that budgets were invented for one reason and that is to exceed them. Your government is the best example.

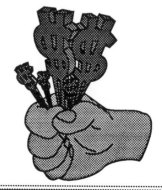

## My wife ran off with my best friend, and I sure miss him

It wasn't many years ago the words "male bonding" had not been heard of. Now phrases like "quality time," "dysfunctional family" and others roll off the lips of experts. In these times of short marriages, a guy needs his pals so it won't be necessary to sleep in his car when she throws him out. A good friend should have a comfortable couch, along with a washer, dryer, TV and a refrigerator stocked with beer. If he doesn't, run an ad for another friend.

# Instead of getting married, just find a woman you don't like and give her your house

I have witnessed several marriages end suddenly, within one week of the ceremony. In both cases this occurred after months of redecorating the groom's house. I'll wager you can guess who is living in the house now and who is sleeping in the car.

A couple of lawyers made a lot of money; the gal and her dog are comfortable in the house, and the guy is asking my bartender what went wrong.

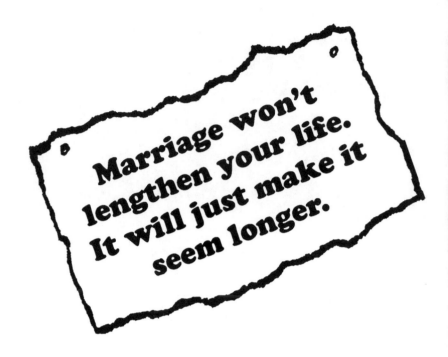

Marriage won't lengthen your life. It will just make it seem longer.

Time seems to come to a standstill when you're not having a good time, or you're just dulling along.

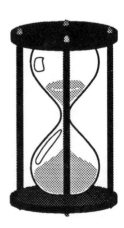

The house needs painting, the yard needs mowing, and the bills are piling up. You'll feel like you're living an eternity.

Learn to walk and talk slowly, and generally aggravate your spouse. Then when you want to go out with the boys, she will be glad you're gone.

**Marriage is the sole cause of divorce**

So simplistic, but that's the way it works, like it or not. I have knowledge of a zillion cases in which couples dated several years, co-habitated and then married. Suddenly the bliss disappears, and the problems really start. Can you explain this to me, it's way over my head. In fact, it's one of the great mysteries of the universe. Call a shrink.

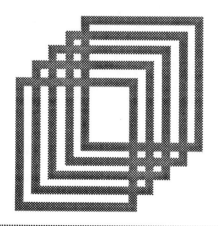

**Marriage is best when you have the flu**

It would be extremely
difficult to disagree with this
sign in the Longbranch Steakhouse.
When bedridden with the flu and its miserable
symptoms, it is important someone else make
the trip to the store for chicken soup, medicine
and magazines. It is also necessary to have
someone running around the house doing many
chores to keep the patient's big mouth shut.
Maybe the one with the flu is the lucky one.

## Marry anyone with a 40-ft. cruiser

The bigger and more expensive the better, but if and when the marriage blows, by all means attempt to retain the boat. Educate yourself to drive and maintain it as soon as possible and previous to dumping your spouse. When you remarry, do not under any circumstances teach your new mate to drive or maintain the boat.

## Marry early in the morning so if it doesn't work out you don't waste the whole day

At first glance, this may seem to be a slight exaggeration, but not as much as you may think. I have personally witnessed many seemingly blissful relationships living together until the dreaded "I do." Of course, if they were living together, they were experiencing the worst part of marriage already. No one ever thinks about bad breath and beer guts, which seem to come after the "I do." None of those things ever happened in Doris Day movies. Could Doris be to blame for marital problems?

**My wife needed more space, so I locked her outside**

I was never informed of the need for space as a young adult, back in the old days. Perhaps the need for it did not exist until the '70s. After all, the whole family usually shared one small bathroom.

The only space my school teachers told me about was "outer." I also knew about parking "space." In the Navy I should have addressed my chief officer and requested more "space," as we were living tightly with 80 guys to a barracks room. I wonder if he would have gotten me a private room, other than a cell?

## The single want to be married; the married want to be dead.

Perhaps a slight exaggeration, but somewhat true in our driven quest to possess what we do not have. Many people I have had the pleasure of encountering along life's way dream of distant places, another occupation, etc. Sort of like the type that flock to new restaurants, while others remain content and comfortable with the old establishments. Sometimes that dream home, different wife and new car will lead you to the house you most want to avoid — the poor house. At times it's best to be miserable with what you have.

# They said it would not last, and we've been married two months

In today's world, people dance in and out of matrimony without batting an eye. When I was a kid stealing hub caps, no one in our Irish Catholic neighborhood considered divorce; they just suffered living together. The losers were obviously the lawyers who finally started an ad campaign to promote divorce so they could afford a new red Mercedes and a divorce.

**10's become 4's after marriage**

Hold it, girls, quit throwing rotten tomatoes at me. I did not mean you on this sign, heaven forbid. I meant the guys. At least that's what I tell 'em in the bar when a female customer becomes irritated and hostile over it. I simply lie to either sex as to whom it is directed. They all seem content with the quote when I inform 'em it's about their mate.

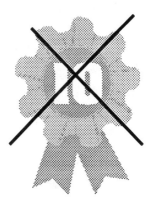

# The Longbranch Story

Before relating the story, I would like to inform you that the Longbranch Steakhouse Saloon is not a high-end, white-tablecloth bar/restaurant, but rather an old eastern-type saloon featuring beef and beer with a few shrimp and various wines thrown in. I have no illusions about the Longbranch, and I wouldn't want you to have any. Though not pretentious, some of the area's wealthiest and most important people eat and drink at the Longbranch. The customer list from pro sports and the world of entertainment is quite lengthy, I am proud to state.

That out of the way, on with the story. By the late '70s I had worked my way through the ranks in the auto business from salesman to majority owner of a Dodge dealership in Kansas City, Kansas. With Chrysler teetering on the brink of bankruptcy, I was fast tiring of the pressure tactics they were using

*Longbranch servers ready to get the place rolling*

*The Longbranch, 9095 Metcalf, with patio customers on a balmy day*

to survive and made the decision to start an old-style saloon in the then dry Overland Park, Kansas, a suburb of Kansas City. At the time it was possible to sell alcoholic beverages if the customer purchased a membership card.

I resigned my stock in the dealership in early 1980, and after prolonged auditing made a peaceful settlement with Chrysler on my equity. It was about the time Lee Iacocca came on the scene for the automaker. In '81 things seemed to start getting better for Chrysler; their stock went from 3 to 35 shortly thereafter. I will always wonder whether it was my departing or Iacocca's arriving that caused the turnaround.

In 1979 Bud Blattner, former Royals announcer, sat in a Plaza restaurant with me discussing what an eastern-type saloon should be and look like. He was also from St. Louis, a town with many locally owned bar/restaurants full of color and character. I valued his opinion, as well as the napkin we drew the plan on.

Soon after that meeting I signed a lease with David Block of Block Management and was ready to start. I arranged a meeting with the architect who slowly inspected the napkin

*Customers enjoy food and beverage at the Longbranch.*

and commented that he had never worked with such an elaborate plan and hoped never to again.

Longbranch opened in April '80, and despite inexperience and more mistakes than I would like to admit, became a hit. In March '81 an opportunity presented itself on the Country Club Plaza. It was a failing bar/pizza operation in the basement of Seville Square, and all my advisors told me not to touch it with a 10-foot pole. Equipped with

*Associate Shiela advises Walt to get a regular job and let her run the Longbranch properly.*

*Ex-Cardinal pitching great Dizzy Dean (left) and Bud Blattner (right) teamed up to announce the TV Game of the Week on CBS in the early '50s.*

more nerve than brains and no funds, I called my old friend and past business partner, Lou Piniella, now a New York Yankee in the twilight of his playing career. Lou had often approached me about entering a business together, and entertained thoughts of retiring in Kansas City. At my request he jumped on a plane, came to town, and we made a partnership deal that lasted until 1993, when I purchased his stock. At the time I was considering retirement, and he had fish to fry in other areas. We remain good friends, and he is currently doing a masterful job for the Seattle Mariners as manager.

The second Longbranch quickly became a favorite on the Plaza with soaring sales; in fact, it was second in sales per square foot in a very competitive area of 28 restaurants.

*Walt plans a private party for a couple of suckers at the Longbranch.*

*Longbranch customers make use of the private party room for an informal get-together.*

"When you're moving well, don't stop," said a belly dancer, so in 1986 I purchased a defunct Peoples Restaurant located in Lenexa, Kansas, also a suburb of Kansas City. The old saloon concept was running smoothly, and by that time my walls were loaded with handwritten sayings, all about real life. The customers enjoyed them, especially the married ones because they could read the signs instead of talking (just kidding).

I realize the new fashionable restaurants serve a purpose and do a good job, but it seems the customers all try to look alike, the cars in the parking lot are similar, and the bill is high, twice as high. At the Longbranch you'll find character, good or bad, and customers from every walk of life. Even the parking lot appears to have a greater range of cars of various colors.

In early '95 I sold my holdings in Lenexa and the Plaza to my loyal long-term managers, retaining the Metcalf location. I enjoy the customers and drop by on a daily basis. It would be great to meet you and have your assistance in writing another famous saying for the walls.

*Lou Piniella, manager Seattle Mariners, a long-time associate and friend of Walt's.*

*Lou Piniella, Walt and Bozo the monkey. The monkey is the one on the left.*

*Better heed Walt's advice when you buy a used car, or you might end up sitting on it in the repair shop instead of driving it.* *(See story on Page 130.)*

*Longbranch servers proudly point out how mean they are.*

*Walt standing behind the bar in front of some famous signs in a $2.00 hat.*

# Love

# Momentary pleasure can bring long-term grief

How long the grief would require a far wiser man than I to tell you, but it is at least 100 times the pleasure. Forget that hot date Saturday night, and instead head for the library, broaden your horizon. On second thought, keep the date, what the hell.

**Jack and Jill went up the hill — and things were never the same again**

God and nature somehow created the universe, with its ice age and hurricanes, famine, even caused a flood so Noah could go boatin'. Adam and Eve were only a minor glitch; the real trouble started when Jack took Jill up that damn hill. I haven't the faintest idea what he did or did not do, but it was the beginning of the women's movement as we know it today.

Thanks, Jack.

# Women don't get heart attacks — they give 'em

Don't argue about this one, ladies, the facts will refute your case. Survey after survey indicates women outlive men. I have checked this out. It's apparent women don't eat better, get more exercise or more rest. It's just this simple — they don't need to put up with being married to a woman. Facts are facts, and I refuse to hear any arguments to the contrary.

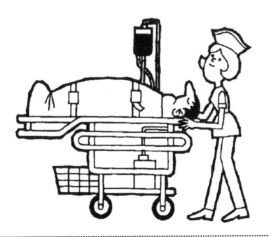

# You will always have a good time with a girl named "Boom-Boom"

... or "Bubbles." Don't bring either of these girls home to meet your mom. None of the educators at your alma mater informed you of that fact of life. Feel free to marry Nancy, Jane or Joan; bring them home to visit anytime. On the other hand, have your dad join you at the local pub to meet "Boom-Boom" and "Bubbles." He will approve and have a hell of a good time. Keep your big mouth shut about the event.

# Someday, somewhere, someone will dump you

It's lurking somewhere in your future. The threat alone sells millions of dollars of exercise equipment on late night TV. Fifty percent of the populace is trying to look good to snare a mate, while the other fifty percent is exercising in the hope they can retain one. Somewhere out there is another fifty percent getting in shape to

dump a mate and then look good. I know these percents don't add up, but they are right.

## Only guilty people send flowers

Darn right they did something wrong, that's why there is a florist shop on every corner. It's impossible for that many guys to like their wives, much less love 'em. On the next occasion you receive flowers or candy, make a list of the ten worst things the rat could have done. A good defense is sometimes the best offense. And visa versa. Anyway, the rat did do something wrong; it's up to you to figure it out.

Love is great —
everyone needs
someone to
argue with

You're aware of that, I'm aware of that.
Think back about how many arguments you
have had with people you don't love or even like.
Very few, right? Pretty darn peaceful life, you
must admit. The unwritten law is you argue
with people you love. It's your way of showing
them how much you care, like sending flowers,
only in reverse.

**Show me a love affair, and I'll show you grief**

Far and away, the most popular sign ever to adorn the walls of the Longbranch Steakhouse, always filled with customer signatures. Should love affairs be this much work, and if so, why? Did we see too many Doris Day movies, plots that always ended well? I have come to the conclusion that Doris Day is the reason for all this turmoil. It's my famous Doris Day theory.

# Kids

# Only kids can open kid-proof lids

Who are those folks that design those tamper-proof packages? The frustration experienced simply trying to open the mouthwash is far worse than having bad gums or breath. Who runs the tests on these things? Is anyone strong enough to open the Hi Ho crackers in the plastic container? I struggled for 30 minutes with the Nyquil bottle and slept well due to exhaustion. I finally discovered the need to push down on the lid, but was too weak to do it.

**Did parents in Arizona walk three miles to school in the snow?**

Every kid's parents did, never met anyone who has not heard that. Did it snow everywhere in the old days? Has global warming taken over? Was San Diego a ski capital in 1930? Makes you wonder. Pass it on, it's part of our folk lore.

**Never let a kid you love drive a car you like**

You know it and I know it. Admit it. Your car was never quite the same after your 16-year-old angel drove it. Sure, he and his six goofy friends just drove slowly around town attempting to pick up girls. Luckily it may look the same, but the car knows it's been through hell. Repair bills will increase next week. An angel drove it.

# Sports

**A coach's lifetime contract means he can't be fired in the 4th quarter if his team is ahead**

The poor, overworked coach — he vacillates from hero to bum, depending on what his team is doing, and his fate can change at the twist of an ankle. Everyone in town second-guesses him, and some want to lynch him. They usually fire him twenty-four hours after they give him a vote of confidence.

# ON SKIING

I don't wish to participate in any sport that keeps an ambulance at the bottom of the hill

The mere thought of hurtling down a hill at breakneck speed sends terror through my body. Don't the dummies realize that beneath that beautiful white cover lie large boulders just waiting to crack their bones. Looking further down the hill, there sits the ambulance crew, secure in the knowledge that you will become a paying customer, sooner or later, probably sooner.

**Never purchase a putter you don't throw first**

Come on, you golf nuts, admit it. It is an extremely frustrating game, invented for the purpose of freeing married guys from their household duties. I have personally observed

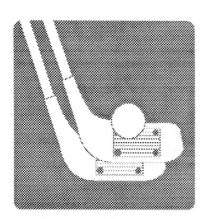

grown men break clubs, cheat, curse and turn blue in the face. An observant person once wrote, "Golf is a good way to ruin an otherwise pleasant stroll in the countryside."

## Horses I follow follow other horses

And usually quite a far distance behind. I seldom experience the pleasure of losing in a photo finish. There seems to be no system I have not employed to taste the agony of defeat. I'll meet you at the paddock next week; I hear the gray horses are running well. We'll make a killing.

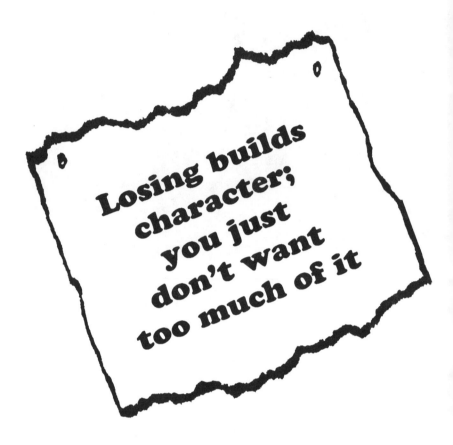

Losing builds character; you just don't want too much of it

The agony of defeat, how sweet it ain't. Casey Stengel once said, "I don't like them fellas who drive in two runs and let in three." Another player said, "When you win, your wife looks like Linda Carter." It boggles the mind to think of what she would look like if he were married to Linda. Keep your thoughts to yourself, gentlemen.

**The fans in this town stick behind their coach — win or tie**

Oh, yes, the saga of the fickle sports fan or nut, which is a more appropriate description. Team play seems to be an emotional outlet for pent-up anger from daily life. Without the Super Bowl, murder could increase 50%. Hometown fans count the injuries on their team as a reason for the gut-wrenching, end-of-the-world defeat, ignoring the fact that their opponent had many more wounded. Finally, fire the coach, the dirty rat, it's the way of the world.

Sports are not a matter of life and death. They are far more important.

Have you ever observed a sports fanatic in the middle of an important sporting event? It's like watching some kind of sadist spotted with mustard, beer and potato chips, not to mention his open fly. The event takes on an importance so monumental nothing going on in the universe carries more meaning. If his team should lose, the sadness will deepen when he pays his bookie, or his wife finds out how much he lost.

# Business

## Always blame your partner

You're darn night, this is the very best method with which to operate a business or a marriage. Why would you want to shoulder the blame? The fact that you forgot and locked the keys in the car does not mean you could possibly be at fault. What kind of dummy would give you the keys to begin with? Charge forward blaming others and never flinch or apologize.

**All stock tips stink**

I know this sign is true. Were it not, I would be lounging on a beach rather than working for a living. I'm sure someone, somehow, in a faraway land made money on a stock tip, but it sure as hell

wasn't me or anyone I am acquainted with. I'm gonna tell you where stock tips come from. They emit from a person who already bought the stock and wants you to purchase it in hopes it will cause it to rise, or a broker with a hot date, looking for a quick commission. After you buy it and drive it up, they will sell their stock, leaving you holding the bag.

When asked why he robbed banks, Willie (the Rat) Sutton replied, "Because that's where the money is."

Willie was a crook and a legend, but a guy with great basic logic. Many of us need to improve ours. He specialized in robbing banks in the eastern section of the United States and so mastered his trade he became a legend. Keep it simple, do it well, and you, too, can become a legend. Just don't end up like Willie unless you like pinstripes.

**Businesses are always best before they open**

A huge understatement before the heartache begins, and also prior to the sleepless nights you lay in bed staring into the unlit ceiling. The new venture will be similar to traveling through a field of land mines. Years later when your enterprise begins to function smoothly, you will hear how lucky you were. Don't tell 'em how tough it was; they would never believe you anyway.
Encourage them to strike out on their own, learning first hand to deal with employees, banks, landlords, customers and federal laws.

### Don't let the boss know you're smarter than she is

Some things are better left unsaid, and this rule of the business world is important to your economic survival. There is an old adage: "The boss may not be right, but the boss is the boss." If you know your brain functions at a level above that of king boss, keep it a well-hidden secret until the right moment, then strike like a snake. Possibly you will become the top dog and others will lurk in the shadows, secure in the knowledge that they are of superior intelligence, and poised to strike like a snake. Sleep with the doors locked and one eye open, remembering they are probably planning to overthrow you in the morning.

Everyone has a plan for getting rich that will not work

I've listened to so many plans that I feel like a qualified expert on ideas to get rich. How do you tell people you think they will most likely lose their investment on the goofy idea? The very best plan is to be born to wealth or marry it, the first of the two being preferable, and staying rich and single you can put two divorce lawyers out of work at the same time.

# Team work allows you to blame someone else

Rarely in my 130 years in business did anyone say, "I screwed the program up!" Almost everyone perceives others involved allowed the breakdown to occur. That's why it's of utmost importance to design plans which will target another for the mistake. Usually someone will miss a  planning meeting, and that is the person

you try to nail. To do this well you must become cunning and devious.

**The man who invented the wheel was dumb. But the guy who invented the other three got rich.**

Got a great idea, big deal! What is important is how you put it to use. If you happen to stumble on a usage for someone else's idea, that's great. You'll appear much smarter than you really are, a goal we should all shoot for.

Remember, if you can't dazzle 'em with your brain, confuse 'em with bull.

# ON LAWYERS

## If we had not had the first one, we would have never needed the rest

If you think new cars are expensive, you haven't hired lawyers in recent months. Most of their time and billing generate from conversing with other lawyers, while attempting to interpret what a legal book says, written by guess who. Without knowing or even trying, they have invented perpetual motion, which results in perpetual billing. And when the tab arrives at your mailbox, you will become acquainted with what the car buying public refers to as "sticker shock."

Talk is cheap until you hire a lawyer

Don't you dare disagree with me on this one. The legal profession charges for allegedly considering your problem at any time, sitting at stop signs, exercising, you name it. Most of us think about our work in off moments; we just can't bill our boss for it. They write material no one can interpret and send a bill for time spent explaining it. There are lawyers I like; I just like 'em a lot better when they are not billing me.

I wonder what lawyers will do in Heaven. I have a feeling they don't want to listen to harp music all day. Who will they sue? Who will they bill? Maybe God has a special legal section. Maybe He won't let 'em in.

Some
Things
I Wish
I'd
Written

**ON EXERCISE**
**Start slow, taper off.**

**I'm on a seafood diet.**
**I see food. I eat it.**

**If you live in the fast lane,**
**you get to the end**
**in a hurry.**

**It's easier to get**
**forgiveness**
**than permission**

**Don't try to keep up with the Joneses; if possible, drag them down to your level.**

**When the going gets tough, the smart get the hell out.**

**Friends may come and friends may go, but enemies accumulate.**

**Start every day with a smile and get it over with.**

Never get in a car with
a stranger unless
he offers you candy.

You can get more
with a gun and a smile
than you can with a smile.

Crime in the streets
doesn't worry me as much
as crime on the sidewalks.

PROVERB:
He who looketh at
women loseth fender.

Be nice to your kids —
they'll choose
your nursing home.

Why is
"abbreviation"
such a long word?

Your kid may be an
honor student, but
you're still a dummy.

# How to Purchase a Used Car and Feel Good

# How to Purchase a Used Car and Feel Good

The purchase of a used car can be one of life's best bargains when compared to buying a new car. A new vehicle depreciates quickly and at a steep rate, making the used model a great value in comparison. Remember, that shiny new car will become a used car in about six months, and the new car smell will disappear, slinking back to the showroom to seduce another new car buyer.

In my previous career in the auto business, I personally purchased over 6,000 used car from various sources, so I believe I am qualified to pass on some helpful tips.

If you're in the market for a car, consider the money involved. The average person purchases about 15 cars in a lifetime, new or used. If he bought used cars that average $10,000, that's $150,000 — big bucks by any standard. Buying new will run that bill to about $375,000 at a price of $25,000 per unit. You can see that used cars start with a gain of over $200,000. There are other new car expenses that will exceed that of a used car, so be prepared to dig deep. These include sales tax, finance charge, license and personal property taxes.

A credible financial publication recently noted that the purchase of new cars versus used would cost an additional $300,000 in the average lifetime. You will probably spend far more on car purchases than your home, so it's worth some planning.

Here is a simple guide that could save you a fortune.

If your Aunt Millie has a low mileage, like-new cream puff and will sell it to you cheap, go for it and burn this plan. If money is no object and you can't do without the new car smell, that's fine, too — go for it.

Here are some simple rules that will serve you well if you wish to pursue a used car purchase.

### Rule 1 — Prepare yourself

Get the proper information. Review the used car classified section to get up to date on the general prices of what you wish to purchase and your trade-in.

Meet with your bank loan officer and discuss rates. He will also have a book to look up used car values.

Then call your insurance man; let him update you on the rates for the car you intend to purchase.

### Rule 2 — Price, Model, Equipment

Decide what you would like in equipment, color, model and year. If possible, do your shopping at new car dealerships, preferably in affluent areas. Dealers that market higher priced new cars generally have better maintained quality trade-ins.

### Rule 3 — Check the car

When you finally locate the car of your dreams, it's inspection time. Carefully look at the interior, starting with the driver's cab, and if it's not in almost showroom condition, find another car. Next, inspect all the gadgets: turn signals, radio, wipers, power seat, etc. Repairs on these items can cost hundreds of bucks.

If you still like it, you're ready for a test drive. Turn the radio off so you can hear any odd sounds in the car. Take it to the nearest highway and drive 65 m.p.h. This will tell you if the front end and wheels are in balance. Gently apply the brakes, checking for noise or pull to the side.

If you're still satisfied, head for a rough road. You won't need to be an expert to tell if the car and shock absorbers handle it well. If you still like it, you're ready to make a deal.

### Rule 4 — You are in charge.

Remember that the seller wants to make a deal as much as you do, so stay cool and let the seller talk.

Inform the seller you have located another car equally as good and are torn between the two. Make an offer about 20% under the price you're willing to pay. Don't be afraid to do this; the seller will not bite you. The seller might surprise you and accept your offer, but he will usually counter with his lower price. Things are moving along in your favor; stay on track.

### Rule 5 — Sign the order.

You like the car and are anxious to purchase. When you agree on a price and before you sign the order, insist it stipulate that the car must pass a mechanical inspection and the deal be approved by your bank loan officer.

Put up no more than a $50 deposit; I don't care what the salesman asks for. *You are the boss.*

Do not purchase a mechanical warranty or credit life, period. You did a good job; congratulate yourself.

If you still wish to pay a small fortune for the new car smell, at least you have an idea what it will cost. If you did a reasonably good job buying the used one, it will look like new, and you will be many thousands richer in a few years.

I certainly hope you enjoyed this book and had some fun reading it. These thoughts were collected over 16 years in the bar business watching life go by. I hope you can happily relate to some of them

Best Wishes
Walt Coffey

# ORDER FORM

*This book is the perfect gift.*

Please send _____ copies of

## "A Bartender's View of Life."

Name _____

Address _____

City/State/Zip _____

Each book is priced $9.95 plus $4.00 for sales tax, packing and shipping. Enclose check (payable to Longbranch) or indicate credit card information.

Bill my: ☐ Visa  ☐ MasterCard

Card No. _____ Exp. Date _____

Your Signature _____

Use this form or photocopy and mail to:
Longbranch
c/o Taschler and Assoc., Suite 100
5931 Nieman Rd.
Shawnee Mission, KS 66203

For information, call (913) 631-5626
Fax order to (913) 631-5965